FATIMA

IN BRIEF

A Treatment for All Ages

by Rev. T. G. Morrow

Catholic Faith Alive!, Inc.
1309 Ridge Road
Pylesville, MD   21132
1-877-324-8492
www.cfalive.org

Every reasonable effort has been made to determine copyright holders of excerpted materials and to secure permissions as needed. If any copyrighted materials have been inadvertently used in this work without proper credit being given in one form or another, please notify Catholic Faith Alive in writing so that future printings of this work may be corrected accordingly.

Copyright © 2017 by T. G. Morrow

All rights reserved. With the exception of short excerpts for critical reviews, no part of this work may be reproduced or transmitted in any form or by any means whatsoever without permission in writing from the publisher. Write:

Catholic Faith Alive!, Inc.
1309 Ridge Road, Pylesville, MD   21132
Toll Free # 1-877-324-8492

ISBN: 978-1546341390

Cover and Illustrations by J. Bradford Johnson

PRINTED IN THE UNITED STATES OF AMERICA

Table of Contents

Preface... 7

Introduction... 9

Chapter One

    The Angel of Peace......................... 13

Chapter Two

    Mary Appears................................ 19

Chapter Three

    June Appearance............................ 27

Chapter Four

    Opposition.................................. 33

Chapter Five

    July Appearance............................ 37

Chapter Six

The Third Secret. 43

Chapter Seven

Trouble with Authorities. 47

Chapter Eight

Captivity. 53

Chapter Nine

August Appearance. 65

Chapter Ten

September Appearance. 69

Chapter Eleven

October Appearance. 73

Chapter Twelve

Anti-Catholic Doings. 81

Chapter Thirteen

Postlogue. 83

The Importance of The Rosary.................... 89

Reflection...................................... 93

Preface

This account of the miracles and message of Our Lady of Fatima was written for children and really, all ages. There are a number of footnotes in the text to guide parents as to which words might not be understood by children.

Introduction

It is just a ten minute walk from Fatima, Portugal to the town of Aljustrel, where was born Lucia Abóbora on March 22, 1907. She was the last of seven children of Antonio Abóbora, owner of a small farm and herd of sheep, who was only mildly religious, and Maria Rosa, his devout[1] wife. In the evenings, Antonio and his older daughters would tell stories about mysterious princesses and haunted castles, but Maria Rosa would always try to work in a word or two about the faith. {W 1-4}

The traditional age for receiving first Communion in Fatima, where the family attended Mass, was about ten. However, Maria Rosa decided that her little Lucia should receive at age six. So, she had eleven-year-old Caroline help her teach her younger sister the catechism, and quiz her to make sure she knew all the answers. Then, the proud mother brought Lucia to St. Anthony's church to be tested by the priest. {W 6, 7}

When she got to the church Fr. Pena began to ask her the

---

[1] Devout means strongly religious.

usual questions: "Who made the world? Why did God make us? What must we do to be saved?" They felt her answers were good. However, after thinking about it for a moment or two, the pastor told them she needed one more year. The two were broken-hearted. First Communion was to be held the next day. {W 7}

They went out into the church and sat in a pew. Lucia started crying. By chance, a visiting priest, Fr. Cruz, was walking by at just that moment, and seeing Lucia sobbing, he asked her what the problem was. When he discovered what had happened, he asked her some of the questions himself. Satisfied with her answers, he marched her right back to the other priest and pointed out, "This girl knows her answers better than some who are going to receive." {W 7}

"But she's only six years old!" replied Fr. Pena. {W 7}

Fr. Cruz refused to give up his cause. He was a kind, humble priest, but he had made up his mind that Lucia should receive, and after a few minutes he was able to convince his brother priest to allow her to do so. Lucia's sadness quickly turned to delight! {W 7}

She would have to go to confession now, her first, so that her soul could be pure when she received the Lord Jesus. She went to her new friend, Fr. Cruz. After she told her tiny sins to the saintly priest, he told her, "My daughter, your soul is the temple of the Holy Spirit. Keep it always pure so He can carry out His divine activity in it." {W 7, 8}

She told him she would and went out to say her penance. She prayed to the Blessed Mother to help her receive Jesus well the following day. She then went over to kneel before the statue of Mary and prayed, "Mary, please keep my poor heart for God." {W 8}

That night her sisters prepared everything: the white dress, the crown of flowers... That night she could hardly sleep, thinking of the big day ahead. {W 8, 9}

Her sister woke her up in the morning and helped her get dressed. Then she brought Lucia to her parents so she could ask forgiveness from them, kiss their hands, and receive their blessing. Once she had received it, her mother told her, "Now don't forget to ask Our Lady to make you a saint." Then they all began their walk to the church. {W 9}

They arrived early, or rather, the Mass was to start late, so Lucia had time to go over to the statue of Our Lady of the Rosary and do as her mother had instructed her. She knelt there and prayed, "Make me a saint. Please ask our Lord to make me a saint!" {W 9}

Soon the procession was coming together and Lucia, as the smallest, was the first in line. The Mass began, and the time came for Holy Communion. The priest put the body of

Christ on her tongue and immediately she experienced a firm sense of "serenity and peace." She went back to her place and knelt. There she prayed, "Lord, make me a saint! Keep my heart always pure, for You alone!" She felt she heard the response, "The grace I grant you today will remain living in your soul, producing fruits of eternal life." {W 10}

When Mass ended, all the other children marched out of church and began to celebrate with their family and friends. Lucia stayed in church a long time. Finally, her mother came to get her and bring her home for lunch. Once there, the young girl had little interest in food. She had received God himself within her. What a blessing! It was several weeks before she descended from what seemed to be a cloud of joy. {W 10}

Chapter One

The Angel of Peace

Lucia had many cousins, but her two favorites were Francisco and Jacinta Marto. She shared with them the job of shepherding the family sheep. One summer morning in 1916 the three were tending their sheep when a rainy mist came up. They moved the sheep to a grove of trees and then entered into a small cave-like shelter nearby. After eating lunch there they said the Rosary. Often they would just say the first two words of the Our Father and Hail Mary when they said their little Rosary, and Lucia was uncertain if this was the case that day. After the Rosary the weather cleared up and they began to pass the time by throwing stones down the hill. {W 11, 35}

Suddenly the trees began to be bent by a powerful wind. They looked up and saw a white light moving across the valley toward them. It seemed to be the same brightness Lucia had seen with friends the year before, but this day it came close. It appeared to be a boy about 15 years old, "transparent, more brilliant than crystal penetrated by the rays of the sun."

The children could hardly move as they stood looking up at the strange being standing above the opening of their little shelter. {W 35, 36}

"Do not be afraid," the being said. "I am the Angel of Peace. Pray with me." He knelt on the ground leaning forward so that his forehead rested on the ground. He prayed, "My God, I believe, I adore, I hope, and I love You! I beg pardon for those who do not believe, do not adore, do not hope and do not love You!" {W 36}

The children, a bit stunned, knelt in imitation of him and prayed along with him as he repeated the prayer three times. Then he said, "Pray in this way. The hearts of Jesus and Mary are awaiting your requests." Then he seemed to melt into the light. {W 37; LS 2}

The three stayed on their knees for some time, as if in a trance, unable to move. They went on reciting the prayer for what seemed like a long time. Finally, little Francisco got tired and sat down. He called to the others to tell them he could not go on kneeling that way any more. It was not long before they came to their senses and were leading the sheep back toward their homes. They hardly said a word as they walked. When they got near home Lucia told the two younger children not to say a word about what had happened. She wasn't sure why she said that, but it just seemed so "intimate" that they should keep it to themselves. {W 37}

It was just weeks later when the angel came again. The three were playing behind Lucia's house, and suddenly he was there. "What are you doing? Pray, pray much!" he said. "The hearts of Jesus and Mary have merciful plans for you. Offer prayers and sacrifices constantly to the Most High [God]." {W 39}

"How do we sacrifice?" asked Lucia. {LS 4}

"With all your power offer a sacrifice in reparation[2] for the sinners by whom He is offended and of prayer for the conversion of sinners. In this way you will bring peace upon your country. I am its Guardian Angel, the Angel of Portugal. Above all accept and endure... the suffering the Lord will send you." Then the angel disappeared again. {W 39, 40}

As before, they were in a kind of daze after he left. Although Francisco had seen the angel he heard not a word. When he asked, Jacinta put him off. It took a couple of days before Lucia had her wits restored as the appearance of the angel had left them somewhat dazed. It was she who finally told him what was said during both visits, but it took him a while to understand about offering sacrifices to make up for

---

[2]Reparation means repairing the damage caused by sin.

sins. Once he caught on, he willingly competed with the other two to give up enjoyments and comforts for sinners. Together they would offer the prayer for hours on end as they lay on the ground face down. {W 40, 41}

It was perhaps two months later, in October, when the angel came again. They had finished the Rosary at the same little cave and then prayed several times together, "My God, I believe, I adore, I hope..." As before, the bright, glowing body came and stood before them, suspended in the air. He had in his hands a chalice and a Host above it, showing it to the children. {W 41}

He left them in mid-air and threw himself face down on the ground in worship. He prayed three times, "Most Holy Trinity, Father, Son, Holy Spirit, I adore you... and I offer you the most precious Body, Blood, Soul and Divinity of Jesus Christ, present in all the tabernacles[3] of the world, in reparation for the [insults], sacrileges[4] and [neglect] with which He Himself is offended. And through the infinite merits of His Most Sacred Heart and of the Immaculate Heart

---

[3] The tabernacle is the beautiful little gold box where the Eucharist is kept after Mass.

[4] A Sacrilege is the misuse of something sacred.

of Mary, I beg of you the conversion of poor sinners." {W 41, 42}

Then he stood up. He again held the chalice and Host in his hands and knelt down on a high rock. He showed them the Host and spoke, "Take and drink the body and blood of Jesus Christ, terribly insulted by ungrateful men. Make reparation for their sins and console your God." {W 42}

He then offered the Host to Lucia who received it on her tongue. He gave the chalice to the younger two to drink. After that he fell to the ground again and, prayed, face down, three more times, "Most Holy Trinity, Father, Son, Holy Spirit, I adore you..." The three prayed it as well. Then he disappeared again into the bright sun. {W 42}

The children were left with a deep peace, but a feeling of weakness as well. When they returned to their senses, they quietly gathered the sheep and brought them home. For some time after that, perhaps weeks, they were in a state of delightful calm. {W 42}

After some weeks, Francisco spoke of the event for the first time. "I like seeing the angel, but the worst part is afterwards we can't do anything. I can't even walk..." {W 42}

Some days later, when he regained his strength he asked Lucia, "The angel gave you Holy Communion, but what did he give me and Jacinta?" {W 42}

"That was Holy Communion too," answered Jacinta, without waiting for Lucia to answer. "Didn't you see it was the blood that fell from the Host?" {W 42, 43}

"I did feel that was God in me, but I just didn't know how." Then the boy fell to the ground and prayed face down the new prayer over and over, "Most holy Trinity..." {W 43}

Thus went the apparitions[5] of the Angel of Peace to the three children, ages nine, eight and six in the summer and fall of 1916. They said nothing of this to anyone. Little did they know, there was much more to come. {W 43, 44}

---

[5] An apparition here is an appearance of someone from heaven.

Chapter Two

Mary Appears

The following spring, 1917 the world was at war, and many feared for the lives of their loved ones, including the brothers of the three little shepherds. On May 13 the children were again tending their sheep when a bright flash appeared near them. Thinking it was lightning, they began to move the sheep down the hill to take refuge under a tree. Then they saw another flash, and they ran from their shelter. Suddenly they saw, above a small holm oak tree, a bright globe with a lovely lady standing in the middle. Lucia described her as "more brilliant than the sun." Her face was absolutely beautiful, "not happy, not sad, but serious." The children could hardly look at her, she was so bright. {W 48-51; P 26}

"Don't be afraid. I won't hurt you," said the beautiful lady. {W 51}

"Where do you come from?" asked Lucia.

"I am from heaven," she answered.

"And what do you want of me?" asked the girl.

"I want you to come here for six months in a row, on the thirteenth day, at this same hour," said the mysterious woman. "Then I will tell you who I am and what I want. And, afterwards I will appear here a seventh time."

"Will I go to heaven too," asked Lucia. {W 51}

"Yes you will," responded the Lady.

"And Jacinta?" she added.

"She will go also."

"And Francisco?"

"He also. But he will have to say many Rosaries."

Lucia then thought of two young neighbors who had just died. "Is Maria de Neves now in heaven?" she asked.

"Yes, she is."

"And Amelia?"

"She will be in purgatory until the end of the world." {W 51}

The Lady then asked, "Do you want to offer yourselves to God, to endure all the suffering he may send you, as an act of reparation[6] for the sins by which He is offended, and to ask for the conversion[7] of sinners?" {W 51, 52}

---

[6]Reparation means repairing the damage caused by sin.

[7]Conversion means turning back to God.

"Yes, we do." {W 52}

"Then you will have much to suffer. But, the grace of God will be your comfort." {W 52}

At that point the lady stretched forth her hands and from them came forth two rays of bright light which seemed to pass into the depths of their being. They felt moved by a strong power outside them to kneel and to pray, "O most holy Trinity, I adore You! My God, my God, I love You in the most Blessed Sacrament!" {W 52}

When they finished this, the lady said, "Pray the Rosary every day to obtain peace for the world, and the end of the war." {W 52}

Then, she began to move gently upward from the evergreen tree and move toward the east. Finally she vanished. {W 52}

Again the children said nothing for quite some time, but unlike the time after the angel's visit, they did not feel weak. Rather they felt almost weightless, ready to float up into the sky. As before, Francisco had seen the vision, but had heard nothing. So, the others told him everything. {W 52, 53}

Lucia warned them both not to speak a word of all this to anyone, not even their parents. They both promised, but Lucia had little confidence in their promises. {W 53}

Alas, Lucia was right. When Jacinta got home and saw her

mother, she ran to her and hugged her. Without thinking, she blurted out, "Mother, I saw Our Lady today at the Cova!" {W 54}

Her mother was amused. She told her daughter, "O yes, you are such a good saint that you see Our Lady!" {W 54}

Again, Jacinta proclaimed, "But I *saw* her," and reported the whole story. She told her about the flash, bright globe, and the lady's request that they pray the rosary daily; and that she and Francisco would go to heaven. Her mother still doubted, but her father thought it quite possible, since the two always told the truth. {W 54-56}

The next morning Lucia's sister said, "O Lucia. I hear you saw Our Lady at the Cova." She told Lucia that Jacinta had told her parents. The word was getting around. Lucia was broken-hearted that her cousin had not kept the secret. It was not long before Lucia was getting a serious talk from her mother for lying. {W 56, 57}

Later, as the children brought out their sheep to pasture, their delight had turned to sadness. They couldn't play. They decided they should say the complete Our Father and Hail Mary when they said the Rosary, rather than just the first two words of each prayer as they had been doing. And, they thought about the sacrifices they were going to offer for sinners. {W 57, 58}

They decided to give their lunches to the poor children who would beg for food. But, by 3 pm they felt as if they were starving, so they started searching for food. They tasted some acorns from an evergreen, and they weren't bad. In fact, Jacinta proclaimed they were too good to be considered a sacrifice. So, she found some others which tasted sour, and endured eating them "for the conversion of sinners." In time they found other things to eat which they found growing wild. {W 58}

One very hot day they went to a nearby house to request some water. Having received it from a kind woman, Lucia offered it to Jacinta and Francisco. But they refused to drink, as a penance to convert sinners. Lucia decided she too would make this sacrifice, and so she emptied the water bottle and brought it back to the woman. {W 59, 60}

At one point Jacinta cried out, "Tell the crickets and frogs to keep quiet, it gives me such a headache!" {W 60}

Francisco asked, "Don't you want to offer this for sinners?" {W 60}

"Yes, I do," she replied. "Let them sing." {W 60}

Meanwhile, Lucia's mother decided she was going to get her daughter to admit her lie about the Lady. She threatened her with all sorts of punishments, but with no effect. So, she brought her to the priest, hoping he could get her to admit to her lie. Again, it had no effect. How could she deny it? It was true! {W 60}

It appeared to Lucia that everyone in the town was angry at her over the vision. As she would walk by, neighbors would talk aloud about her, and children would taunt her about Mary appearing. Even her sisters would make fun of her. Francisco was a great help to her during these trials. He was more than willing to suffer for souls. He said, "Our Lady told us we would have much to suffer. That doesn't matter to me. I will suffer everything, as much as she wants!" Sometimes when Lucia was about to cry, Francisco would console her by saying, "Didn't Our Lady say we would have much to suffer?" This helped her to be strong. {W 60, 61}

Once two priests came to see Lucia. They spoke kind words to her, which helped raise her spirits, and requested that she "pray for the Holy Father." {W 61}

"Who is the Holy Father?" she asked. They told her he was the Pope, the head of the Church. After that the three prayed three extra Hail Marys for the Holy Father whenever they prayed the Rosary. {W 61}

Francisco began to want to be alone more for prayer, as he began to fulfill Mary's requests and grow in holiness. He would work his way to the top of a large rock and lie there without moving. When it came time for the Rosary and the boy did not want to come down, the girls would climb up to pray with him. "What were you doing all this time?" they asked. {W 61, 62}

"I was thinking of God, who is so sad because of so many sins," he replied. "If only I could give Him some joy!" {W 62}

Chapter Three

June Appearance

As June 13 approached the children were eagerly looking forward to fulfilling Mary's instructions. Lucia's mother, Maria Rosa, looked forward to the 13th as well, because it was St. Anthony's feast. This was a day which delighted the children. There were special foods, singing, and fire-works, not to mention the special Mass and procession at the church. Maria Rosa and her other children were certain that this grand event would make Lucia give up her lie about the Blessed Virgin appearing. {W 62, 63}

On the evening of June 12 the family spoke in glowing terms about the wonderful events of the following day. Lucia kept quiet. When they made her respond, she said confidently, "I am going to the Cova tomorrow. That is what the Lady wants." Her mother replied, "We'll see if you leave the feast to go talk to that Lady!" {W 63}

Maria Rosa would have prevented Lucia from going had she not gotten advice from the new parish priest, Fr. Manuel.

"Let them go if they persist," he said, "and see what happens. Then bring them to me and I will question them. We'll get to the bottom of this yet!" {W 64}

On June 13 Lucia had the sheep out grazing before dawn, so she could return and go attend Mass at 10 am. After some time in the fields her brother Antonio raced out to let her know she had visitors at home. Some people apparently had heard of the apparition and wanted to attend. She left her brother to take care of the sheep and ran home. Although she was unhappy about their coming, she told them that if they were there when she came back from Mass they could go with her. It seems they didn't think of going to Mass with her! {W 65}

The little girl was back from Mass in about two hours, and at around 11 am she set out with all these people following her. As she walked to her cousins' house she was feeling very sad after hearing all the unkind remarks of her family. Having to answer all the questions of these pilgrims did not help either. She started to cry as she made her way to her cousins' house. {W 65, 66}

When she got there Jacinta told her, "Don't cry! Surely these must be the sacrifices the angel said God would send us. That is why you suffer–and to make reparation to Him, and convert sinners!" Lucia wiped away her tears and off they went. {W 66}

When they arrived at the Cova there were more than fifty people waiting to see what might happen. The three sat down and after a few moments, prayed the Rosary. Shortly after that Lucia shouted, "Jacinta, there comes Our Lady. There is the light!" {W 66, 67}

When Mary arrived, Lucia said, "You asked me to come here. Please tell me what you want." {DM 66}

Mary responded, "I want you to come here on the thirteenth day of next month, to pray five decades of the Rosary every day, and to learn to read. I will tell you later what I want." {W 68; DM 67}

Lucia then requested that Mary heal someone whose name she had been given. Mary answered, "If he is converted, he will be healed during the year." {W 68}

"I would like to ask you to take us to heaven," continued Lucia. {W 68; LS 14}

"Yes, Jacinta and Francisco I will take soon. But you remain here for some time longer. Jesus wishes to make use of you to make me known and loved. He wants to establish devotion to my Immaculate Heart[8] in the world. I promise salvation to those who embrace it, and those souls will be loved by God like flowers placed by me to adorn His throne." {LS 14, 15; W 68}

"I stay here? Alone?" {W 68}

"No, my daughter. Are you suffering a great deal? Don't lose heart. I will never leave you. My Immaculate Heart will be your protection, and the way that will lead you to God." {LS 15; W 68}

Then Mary opened her fingers, and as before, two beams of light came forth from her hands and enfolded the children. They felt as if they were "immersed in God," as Lucia later described it. Jacinta and Francisco, said Lucia, "seemed to be in that part of the light that rose towards heaven, and I in that which was poured out on the earth. In front of the palm of Our Lady's right hand was a heart encircled by thorns which pierced it. We understood that this was the Immaculate Heart of Mary, outraged by the sins of humanity, and seeking reparation." {LS 15}

---

[8]Devotion to Mary's Immaculate Heart means that people will seek Mary's prayers, knowing the great love Mary has for us in her heart. This would be a bit like devotion to the Sacred Heart of Jesus, only on a smaller scale, since Jesus is God, and Mary is a creature.

Then the children saw Jesus and Mary in that light of God in which they were submerged. Lucia said that Mary appeared "serious." Francisco, however, felt Jesus appeared extremely sad. At this point Mary moved off to the east and disappeared. {W 69}

The people had seen nothing of the Blessed Mother, but they did see the leaves on the evergreen bush somewhat bent as if she had brushed them down slightly as she left. They were quite stirred by all this and began to ask the children about the vision. One urged, "Let's pray the Rosary," and someone else, "No, the Litany. We have to say the Rosary on the way home." After praying the litany of Our Lady, the crowd begin to leave, a few at a time, praying as they walked along. {W 69, 70; DM 68}

It was 4 pm before the children started to return home. Some of the people who had not yet left asked them sarcastic questions as they were leaving, which became rather annoying. For those who asked what Mary had said, the three finally settled on the answer, "It's a secret. I can't talk about it." {W 70; DM 69}

Again, Francisco had seen Mary, but had heard nothing so he had to be filled in about what Our Lady had said. When he learned he and Jacinta would go to heaven soon he was delighted, and began repeating, "Jacinta and I are going to heaven soon! Heaven, heaven!" {W 70, 71}

Chapter Four

Opposition

When the two younger ones got home Jacinta announced, "We saw the Lady again, mother. She said I'm going to heaven soon!" {W 71}

"Nonsense!" Olimpia Marto replied, and then asked some questions about "the Lady." "Well, what did she tell you this time?" {W 72}

"To say the Rosary and to go every month till October," the little girl answered. {W 72}

"Is that all?" asked her mother. {W 72}

"The rest is a secret." {W 72}

Then, they all tried to get the secret out of the two, but they refused to say another word. Their father, Manuel Marto, was the only one who did not try to learn the secret, saying, "A secret is a secret, and it has to be kept." {W 72}

Lucia had a much harder time at home than her two cousins. Her mother, Maria Rosa, was certain she was lying, and was embarrassed to learn that fifty people had been so silly as to attend this childish prank. It got even worse when Lucia asked to go to school so she could learn to read as the Lady had requested. Her mother wouldn't hear of it. And, remembering the pastor's suggestion, she told the girl, "Tomorrow we are going to see the priest. And this time you will tell him the truth!" {W 72, 73}

The father of Jacinta and Francisco also arranged for the children to go see the priest. Lucia told her little friends "Tomorrow we are going to see the priest. I am to go with mother and the others are doing their best to scare me about it." Jacinta replied, "We're going too... Never mind. If they beat us we can suffer for Our Lord and for sinners." {DM 71}

The next morning, the three were off, led by Lucia's mother, Maria Rosa. After attending Mass, which was a great comfort to poor Lucia who was so upset, they went directly to the rectory. There the priest asked Lucia a number of questions, to compare her response to those of Jacinta and Francisco. Once he finished his questioning he was satisfied that they were telling the truth. {DM 72; W 74, 75}

He told Maria Rosa, "It doesn't seem to be a message from heaven. It may be a trick of the devil... We will give our opinion later on." {W 75; DM 72}

Lucia now became sadder than ever. Could it have been the devil? She began to doubt everything. Her mother treated her worse now than before, hitting her and even kicking her at times. Feeling scorned in her own house, she made her way out to the old well where the angel had appeared. Her young friends were already there, praying for her. The two would have none of the priest's suggestion that it might be the devil. They consoled her, and continued to do so over the following weeks, but poor Lucia suffered nonetheless. The rejection by her family, and now by the priest, was a great cross. Was he perhaps right? Could this really be from the devil? {W 75, 76}

When July 12 arrived, Lucia wanted no more of this. She told Jacinta and Francisco she would not be going to the Cova. Cries of protest were followed by arguments back and forth. "How can you think it was the devil? Francisco asked. "Didn't you see Our Lady and Our Lord in that great light? And, how can we go without you if you are the one who has to talk?" {W 76, 77}

"I'm not going," was Lucia's answer. {W 77}

"Well, I'm going," Francisco said with certainty.

"And so am I," Jacinta added, "because that Lady told us to."

After some more arguments, Lucia repeated her final verdict, "I'm not going. I told you I'm never going again." {W 77}

The next day Maria Rosa was happy to see her daughter Lucia did not make any move to go to the Cova. However, as the morning wore on, Lucia had a strong urge to go and visit her cousins. When she got to their house she found them kneeling together by Jacinta's bed, praying and crying. {W 77; DM 75; P 56}

Chapter Five

July Appearance

"Aren't you going?" Lucia asked. {W 77}

"We wouldn't dare go without you," they cried. "Come, Lucia, come!" {DM 75}

"I'll come." {W 77; DM 75}

The two went from sadness to delight in a split second. As they stood up, Francisco told her, "I didn't sleep at all last night. I spent the whole night crying and praying that Our Lady would make you go," and off they went. {W 77; P 56}

This time there were between 2,000 and 3,000 people waiting for them when they arrived. Among the crowd was a most devout man from a nearby town who had told the priest his theory about the devil was way off. Why would the devil urge anyone to pray? Manuel Marto, the father of Jacinta and Francisco decided to come as well to observe the events. And, along came Olimpia Marto and Lucia's mother, Maria Rosa, with blessed candles to ward off the devil and to protect the children. Afraid of what others might think seeing them there, they observed everything from a hiding place. {W 78, 79; DM 75, 76}

By the time their parents arrived the three were praying the Rosary in the midst of the crowd of people. They completely ignored a nasty woman who was calling them liars. They finished the Rosary and then, all of a sudden, Lucia said, "Take off your hats! Take off your hats... I see Our Lady already!" Manuel Marto later described what he saw: "...I saw what looked like a little greyish cloud resting on the oak tree and the sun's heat lessened, and there was a delicious fresh breeze... then I began to hear a sound, a little buzzing, rather like a mosquito in an empty bottle." Lucia and her cousins, meanwhile, were looking above the holm oak tree where Mary had arrived. {W 79, 80; DM 76}

"What do you want of me?" Lucia asked again. {W 80; P 59; DM 77}

"I want you to come here on the thirteenth day of the coming month and to continue to say five decades of the Rosary every day in honor of Our Lady of The Rosary to obtain peace in the world and an end to the war, for only she can obtain it." {W 80; DM 77}

Lucia spoke up then, "I want you to tell us who you are, and to perform a miracle so that everyone will believe that you have appeared to us." {W 80}

"Continue coming here every month," answered the Lady. "In October I will tell you who I am and what I want, and I will perform a miracle that everyone will have to believe." {W 80}

Lucia then asked for some healings, including that of a young crippled friend. Mary replied that he would not be healed, but she would help him find work to support himself if he would pray the Rosary daily. Our Lady was quite strong in calling on people to pray the Rosary each day to receive graces. {W 80}

"Sacrifice yourselves for sinners," Mary added, "and say often, especially when you make a sacrifice, 'O Jesus, it is for your love, for the conversion of sinners, and in reparation for the sins committed against the Immaculate Heart of Mary.'" {W 80}

As Mary finished saying this she opened her hands again and sent forth brilliant rays which now entered into the ground, showing below, as Lucia put it, "a sea of fire, and plunged into this fire the demons and souls, as if they were red-hot coals, transparent and black or bronze-colored, with human forms. They floated around in the fire, lifted up by the flames which came from it with clouds of smoke, falling on all sides as sparks from a great fire... [There were] shrieks and groans of sorrow and hopelessness which horrify... The devils appeared with horrible and disgusting forms of animals, frightful and unknown, but transparent like black coals that have turned red-hot." {W 80, 81; LS 17, 19}

The three later said that if Mary had not promised them heaven, they might have died on the spot, so afraid were they. After having been almost glued to this frightening sight, they looked up to the Lady for some comfort. She said to them sadly but kindly, "You see hell, where the soul of poor sinners go. To save them God wants to establish in the world devotion to my Immaculate Heart. If people do what I tell you, many souls will be saved and there will be peace. The war will end. But, if they do not stop offending God, another and worse war will begin in the reign of Pope Pius XI. {W 81}

"When you see the sky lit up by an unknown light, know that it is the great sign that God gives you that He will punish the world for its crimes. [This will come about] by means of war, hunger, and persecution[9] of the Church and the Holy Father.

"To prevent this, I have come to ask for the consecration of Russia to my Immaculate Heart and the Communion of

---

[9] A persecution is an activity which causes pain and misery to another.

reparation on the first Saturdays. If they respond to my requests, Russia will be converted and there will be peace. If not, she will spread her errors throughout the world, causing wars and persecutions of the Church. The good will be martyred, the Holy Father will have much to suffer, and various nations will be destroyed. {W 81, 82}

"In the end my Immaculate Heart will triumph. The Holy Father will consecrate Russia to me, it will be converted and a certain time of peace will be granted to the world. In Portugal, the... faith will always be kept. Do not tell this to anyone... Francisco, yes, you may tell him. {W 82}

"When you pray the Rosary, say after each mystery, 'O my Jesus, forgive us our sins, save us from the fire of hell, and lead all souls to heaven, especially those who are most in need.'" {W 82; LS 20}

The Lady then gave the children the "third secret of Fatima," which was revealed 83 years later, in the year 2000. After this there was silence for some time. Then Lucia asked, "Do you want anything more of me?"

"No, I want nothing more of you today," said Mary. Then she gave the children one more tender look and moved off to the east. So ended what might be considered the most important of Mary's six appearances. {W 83; LS 21}

The people began to close in on the three children and ask

them questions. "What did she look like?" "What did she say?" When they asked why Lucia looked so sad, she kept saying, "It's a secret, it's a secret." Seeing all this was upsetting the children, Manuel Marto made his way through the crowd and lifted up his daughter Jacinta and carried her out to the road. Two other strong men carried the other two behind him. When someone offered them a ride in their car, all four gladly accepted. {W 83; DM 79, 80}

Chapter Six

The Third Secret

What was the third secret? Lucia described it as follows:

...at the left of Our Lady and a little above, we saw an Angel with a flaming sword in his left hand; flashing, it gave out flames that looked as though they would set the world on fire; but they died out in contact with the [brightness] that Our Lady radiated towards him from her right hand. Pointing to the earth with his right hand, the Angel cried out in a loud voice: 'Penance, Penance, Penance!'. And we saw in [a great] light that is God... a bishop dressed in white. We had the impression that it was the Holy Father. Other bishops, priests, men and women religious were going up a steep mountain. At the top there was a big cross of rough trunks as of a cork-tree with the bark.

Before reaching there the Holy Father passed through a big city half in ruins and half trembling, with halting step. [Enduring] pain and sorrow, he prayed for the souls of the [bodies he saw] on his way. Having reached the top of the mountain, as he knelt at the foot of the big cross he was killed by a group of soldiers. They fired bullets and arrows at him. In the same way the other bishops, priests, men and women religious, and various lay people of different ranks and positions died there, one after another.

Beneath the two arms of the cross there were two angels. Each had a crystal [container] in his hand, in which they gathered up the blood of the Martyrs. With it they sprinkled the souls that were making their way to God. {CDF}

The Pope's Secretary of State, Cardinal Angelo Sodano, commented on this third secret as follows on 13 May 2000:

The vision of Fatima concerns above all the war waged by atheistic systems against the Church and Christians, and it describes the great suffering endured by the witnesses of the faith in the last century... It is an endless Way of the Cross led by the Popes of the twentieth century. According to the interpretation of the "little shepherds", which was also confirmed recently by

Sister Lucia, "the Bishop clothed in white" who prays for all the faithful is the Pope. As he makes his way with great difficulty towards the Cross amid the [dead bodies] of those who were martyred (bishops, priests, men and women religious and many lay people), he too falls to the ground, apparently dead, under a hail of gunfire.

The same Cardinal hinted that the events of the third secret of Fatima seemed to be part of the past. He implied that the attack on the Pope may have referred to the attempt to kill Pope John Paul II on 13 May 1981. {CDF}

And, what of the consecration of Russia to the Immaculate Heart of Mary? In a letter she wrote in November 1984, Lucia said the consecration of the world to the Immaculate Heart of Mary which Pope John Paul II made on 25 March 1984 corresponded to Mary's request. {CDF}

Chapter Seven

Trouble with Authorities

The word of the July apparition spread rapidly. Diocesan papers mentioned it, without taking a position as to whether it was real or not. The daily newspapers spoke of it as well, but in a negative way. They sarcastically suggested the people's minds were playing tricks on them, or that the priests had made up the story to get some recognition. {W 84}

The children knew nothing of these news reports, but they had to deal with all sorts of people coming to their house to ask questions or to ask for prayers and cures. Some of the visitors would ask silly questions such as, "Did Our Lady ever eat potatoes?" which made it most difficult for the children to be patient. One wealthy group traveling by car, stopped the children as they walked along the road not far from their houses. They asked, "Where do the little shepherds live? The ones who saw Our Lady?" {W 84, 85}

The children provided them detailed information to get to their houses. Then, as the visitors drove off, the children climbed over the wall by the road and hid behind the trees, delighted with their little trick. {W 85}

The priests who came asked some of the most difficult questions. The children would hide whenever they saw a priest approaching, having had several unpleasant experiences with them. Several were intent on finding flaws in their story. One bright spot among the priests was the Jesuit, Father Cruz, who four years before had helped Lucia receive permission to receive first Communion at the age of six. He was old and bent over, but had the strength to go with them to the Cova and have them replay the events for him. When they finished, he became their friend, and a firm believer in the apparitions. {W 85, 86; P 65}

Not so Lucia's father Antonio. He was most upset when he noticed all the visitors had trampled down his vegetable gardens at the Cova, so that it was impossible to plant anything there anymore. The other family members seemed to be constantly angry at Lucia, since, with the garden ruined, there was not enough food to eat. If Lucia admitted she was hungry, her sisters would taunt her, "Go and eat what you find growing at the Cova!" Or, her mother would comment, "Yes, ask that lady to give you something to eat! You made all those people go to the Cova... Get your food there." Lucia was often hungry, especially at night, afraid to ask anything of her mother, who would often beat her with a stick. Despite all this, Lucia wrote that "by a special grace from Our Lord" she never resented her mother, seeing in her sufferings "the hand of God." {W 86, 87; FLW 75}

The children found a little relief from the constant stress only when they went off to tend their sheep near the Cova. There they would often speak of the vision of hell. Jacinta would ask Lucia, "Doesn't hell end even after many, many, *many* years?" {W 87, 88}

"No," Lucia would reply. {W 88}

Jacinta would say most seriously, "And those people who have to burn there never die? Never? And they never turn to ashes? And if people pray a great deal for sinners the Lord will save them from that? ...we have to pray and make many sacrifices for them!" From this point on Jacinta had a powerful hunger for penance, to save souls from the horror she had seen with her own eyes.

Sometimes she would be lost in thought and Lucia asked what she was thinking. Jacinta responded, "Of that war that is going to come, and of so many people who are going to die and go to hell. What a pity there must be a war and they must go to hell because they won't stop sinning!" {W 88, 89}

She would tell her parents, who had drifted away from the family rosary, that Mary expected families to pray the daily rosary together. After she kept urging them for some time, the parents gave in and picked it up again, and were glad they did. {W 93}

As the August date approached, trouble with the authorities began to brew for the children. The Mayor of Ourem county in which they lived sent letters to their fathers. They were to bring their children, who had caused such a commotion among the people, to appear at court on Saturday, August 11. This was a nine mile trip from the children's homes. The mayor, Arthur Santos, was a great enemy of religion and the most powerful man in the area. Just about everyone feared this man. {W 94, 96, 97; P 70; FLW 74}

Everyone but Manuel Marto, it seemed. He decided to go without his children and speak for them himself. It was much too far for his children to travel. When Lucia and her father arrived at the Marto house the morning of the meeting, Ti was casually finishing his breakfast. Once she heard her cousins were not going, Lucia rushed into Jacinta's room to speak to her. Jacinta told her, "If they kill you, tell them that I am like you, and Francisco even more so, and we want to be killed too. Now I will go with Francisco to the well to pray very hard for you." {W 97, 98; FLW 74}

Lucia wondered at the kindness her cousins received from their parents, while she received anything but kindness. But then she told herself, "But, I must be patient. ...I have the happiness of suffering more for love of You, O my God, and for the conversion of sinners." To add to her misery of having to travel so far, she fell off the donkey three times as they traveled along. {FLW 74; W 99}

When the two fathers and Lucia arrived in the town, the mayor asked her all about the events in the Cova. Then he tried to get the secret out of her, but she refused to talk. The mayor asked Lucia's father, "Do they believe these things over in Fatima?" {W 100}

"Oh no, sir! All this is just women's tales." {W 100}

"And what do you say? ...Do you think it is true?" the mayor asked Manuel Marto. {W 100}

"Yes sir. I believe what they say." At this the mayor and his officials all burst out laughing. Manuel Marto remained calm, having no fear of these men. After a time they were told they could go. As they were leaving the mayor told Lucia, "If you don't tell that secret it will cost you your life." This upset her a great deal. {W 100, 101; FLW 74, 75}

Chapter Eight

Captivity

But, the mayor was not finished. On August 13, the morning of the next appearance by Mary, the Mayor went to the Marto home and told them, "I also want to go to the miracle." Manuel Marto watched as the mayor looked nervously around the room, like someone who has just told a whopping lie. "We might as well all go together. The children can come with me in my carriage." {P 74, 75; W 103}

At that point the children entered the house and the Mayor announced his plan to them. The children said they did not need a ride, but the Mayor insisted. When he got nowhere, he thought of a way to make them ride with him. He told them he wanted to meet with them at the church rectory where he wanted to question the children in the presence of the pastor. They could walk the half mile up the hill, and he would meet them there. To this they agreed. {P 75, 76; W 103}

When they all arrived, the Mayor called Lucia to go in to the priest first. He was most willing to question the girl in front of the mayor, to make it clear that he was not encouraging any of this. He asked her, "Who taught you to say the things you go about saying?" {P 76, 77; W 104}

"That Lady whom I saw at the Cova," Lucia replied.

"Anyone who goes around spreading such lies... will be judged and will go to hell if what they say is a lie. This is more true in your case since so many people go to the Cova because they have been fooled by you." {P 77}

This was a hard thing for Lucia to hear from a man she so respected. But, her response was firm. "If a person who lies goes to hell, I will not go to hell because I do not lie. I simply tell what I have seen, and what the Lady has said to me," said the 10-year-old, without a trace of fear. "And as for the crowd that goes there, they only go because they want to. We don't invite anyone." {P 77; W 104}

The priest had to be a bit awed by the self-assured answer of this ten-year-old girl. "Is it true that the lady gave you a secret?" asked the priest. {P 77}

"Yes, Father." {W 104; P 77}

"Tell it then." {W 104}

"I can't tell it. But if you want to know it I will ask the Lady. If she gives permission I will tell you," said little Lucia. {W 104; P 77}

At that point, seeing that all this was going nowhere, and

in fact, the girl seemed to be sounding more reasonable than the priest, the Mayor interrupted and said they must leave. He led Lucia out and ordered all three into the wagon. The driver immediately took off. But they went in the wrong direction. "You're going the wrong way!" Lucia shouted out. {W 104, 105; P 77}

The Mayor answered, "It's all right. We'll stop and see the priest at Ourem for a moment. Then I'll take you to the Cova by automobile. You'll be there in time." He covered the children with blankets, so the crowd would not see his kidnaping. {W 105}

The two fathers assumed the Mayor was planning to get there another way, so they set off for the Cova. When they got there they were amazed to discover over 6,000 people waiting for the apparition. Some had traveled barefoot for three days to ask a favor of the Blessed Mother. Some others came by mules or horses or bicycles and a few by carriages or cars. As the twelve o'clock hour approached, many began to ask where the children were, but no one had an answer. {W 105}

At about noon a group began praying the Rosary, and soon they were all praying together. After some time they heard a faint buzzing, and then, thunder. Some were fearful and ran off. The others stayed, but in fear. Then they saw a momentary bright flash, like a flashbulb of a camera. The sun dimmed. After that a small, soft, white cloud appeared high in the sky and descended slowly and stopped just over the holm oak tree. After a very short time, it moved upward again and disappeared in the east. {W 106}

After this the clouds were transformed from white to red, then yellow, then blue and every other color. The colors were reflected in the faces of the people and in the trees and landscape. Then, all of a sudden, the sun's brightness returned, as did the whiteness of the clouds. {P 82; W 106}

After this several people came to tell the crowd that the mayor had kidnaped the children and had brought them to the Pastor at Fatima and after that to his home. They became very angry at the news and, thinking their priest part of the plot, began to shout, "Down with the Mayor! Down with the Pastor!" They began to march angrily toward Fatima to take care of the pastor first. {W 106, 107}

However, Manuel Marto stood before them and shouted out, "C'mon now, calm down. Let's not hurt anyone. Let [God] settle this. He will see to it that those who deserve punishment will get it. The whole affair is in His hands." The people were not convinced by his arguments, so they started out toward Fatima. However, by a strange grace, they became calm by the time they reached there, and no harm was done. {P 83, 84}

Meanwhile, when she discovered the kidnaping, Olimpia Marto had run to tell Lucia's mother what had happened to their children. Maria Rosa was not so upset as Olimpia. "It'll teach them a lesson if they're lying." she said. "And, if they're not, Our Lady will take care of them." Olimpia cried and cried. {DM 94, 95}

When the mayor had gotten the children to Ourem, he had said, "I told you I'd win out didn't I? Now you are my prisoners, and you will stay locked up in this room until you reveal the secret." After that, the children had watched the time tick away. As noon had came and gone they had looked at each other nervously. After a few moments Francisco spoke up, "Perhaps Our Lady will appear to us here!" They waited, but she didn't come. After it was clear that Mary was not coming, Francisco said, "Our Lady must be sad because we didn't go to the Cova, and she won't appear to us any more, will she?" he asked of Lucia. {P 79; W 108}

Lucia responded, "I don't know... I think she will." {W 108}

Jacinta began to cry uncontrollably at the thought that Mary was not coming. She sobbed also about her family, "Our parents will never see us again!" {W 108}

"Don't cry," Francisco said. "Let's offer this to Jesus for poor sinners as the Lady told us to do." He looked up toward heaven and prayed, "My Jesus, it is for your love, and for the conversion of sinners!" {W 109}

"And for the Holy Father too!" Jacinta added, "And in reparation for the sins against the Immaculate Heart of Mary!" This thought helped her to dry her tears and be strong... for the time being. {W 109}

After a time, the mayor's wife, a kindly women, had entered the room and said to them, "Don't be afraid. You must be very hungry. I will give you a nice lunch and then you will feel better. And when you finish eating, you can play with my children..." {P 79}

The Mayor kept them there for the night, and the next morning an elderly woman came in and ever-so-gently tried to get the secret out of the children. But she failed. {P 87}

At about ten a.m. the mayor brought them over to the town hall to ask them more of the same questions. On the way over to his office the children were blessed to meet a friendly priest, who listened with great kindness to their story of the previous day. {P 87, 88}

The mayor used every trick in the book to get them to talk, including offering them some gold coins for the information, but the children didn't buy it. This went on for two hours, and again, the mayor had to give up. After the questioning they were completely worn out, and they were brought back to the

Mayor's house, where his wife had prepared a nice lunch for them. {P 88; W 109}

After lunch the Mayor told them they would not be released until they made a confession to end the religious excitement. He then proceeded to put them in the town jail. It was a dark, smelly place. They were put in a room with the petty crooks of the town. Jacinta cried, saying, "We are going to die without ever seeing our parents again. I want to see my mother!" {W 109, 110; P 89 }

Francisco chimed in, "If we never see our mother again, patience! Let us offer it for the conversion of sinners. The worst will be if Our Lady never comes back again... But I'm going to offer that too, for the conversion of sinners." The boy then folded his hands in prayer and said, "O Jesus, it is for love of you and the conversion of sinners." Despite Francisco's courage, later he was bothered by the thought that Our Lady would not come back, and the girls had to encourage him. {W 110; P 89}

The other prisoners began to ask them how they got there. When they heard it, one commented, "Don't be so upset. All you have to do is tell the mayor your secret and he will set you free." Another prisoner chimed in with the same idea. Jacinta answered them with conviction, "That! never! I would rather die than do that!" Francisco and Lucia nodded in agreement. {P 89; W 111}

The other prisoners told Jacinta they didn't want her to cry. "How about if we sing for a while, men? Perhaps that will cheer up our little friends." All agreed and the joyful songs began. One pulled out a harmonica and began to play, and this comforted Jacinta enough to stop crying. Then one of the prisoners asked if the children could dance. Indeed they could, and in a few moments all the children were dancing with the prisoners in a wild, noisy celebration. {P 90; W 112}

After the merriment calmed down, Francisco said, "Let's pray the Rosary!" Jacinta asked one of the inmates to hang up her medal on the wall, which he did. Then the three knelt down and with their eyes focused on Jacinta's medal, they began to pray. Some of the other prisoners were moved by all this and they too knelt and prayed with the children. Even those not devout enough to kneel began to say some of the prayers in a low voice. {P 90; W 111, 112}

Francisco stopped for a moment, and looking at one of the prisoners remarked, "When people pray they can't keep their hats on." The man took it off immediately and threw it down. Francisco, wanting things to be orderly, took it from the floor and put it on a chair, as he continued to pray. {W 112}

When they finished all were quiet for a moment. Then, Jacinta started crying again. When Lucia asked if she didn't want to offer this for the conversion of sinners, she said, "Yes, but whenever I think of my mother, I can't help crying." {P 91}

At last, they were interrupted by a policeman who entered their cell told the children "Come with me." He brought them to the Mayor's office. The Mayor asked once more, "Are you going to tell me the secret?" {P 91}

"No," they all said. {P 91}

"Well, I'm finished fooling with you. If you don't tell me the secret I'm going to boil you all in oil." Then a nasty looking guard appeared. The Mayor asked, "Is the oil good and hot?" {P 91, 92; W 113}

"Yes sir." {W 113}

"Boiling?"

"Yes sir." {W 113}

"Take this one and throw her in," he said, pointing to Jacinta. The guard led her off. {W 113}

Francisco and Lucia were left to pray for little Jacinta. Francisco prayed she would die before she would tell the secret. Then he said to Lucia, "What do we care if they kill us? Then we'll go straight to heaven." {W 113}

Shortly the mean-looking guard returned. "She's fried. Now for the next one," he proclaimed. And, he took Francisco away. {W 113}

The Mayor, now all alone with Lucia, said, "You'll be next. You'd better tell me the secret."

"I'd rather die," she replied. {W 113}

"And so you will." {W 113}

Soon they led Lucia down a hallway to a room where she discovered her two friends, alive and well. How happy they were to see each other! The Mayor's little trick had backfired. The children had won! {W 114}

He held them there another night in his house, and the next day he questioned them some more. Again unable to get the secret, he brought them home. While driving them home, the mayor tried one last trick. He told them, "I'm taking you children home now, but if you ever return to the Cova, I will come and get you and bring you back to Ourem." The day they were released was August 15, the feast of the Assumption, when Mary was raised up to heaven, body and soul. It was a lovely feast-day present from Mary. {W 114; P 93, 94}

The Mayor brought them to Fatima and delivered them to the rectory porch, knowing their parents would soon be coming out of the feast day Mass. There their worried parents found them as they came out of the church. When the crowd leaving Mass realized that the children had just been released from a two-day kidnaping, they became angry. Again, as a few days before, the crowd began to yell against the Mayor and the Pastor. Again, Manuel Marto calmed them down. {W 115}

Before returning home the children went to the Cova to pray the Rosary before the little tree. They all returned home after that, happy to be delivered from the evil Mayor. {W 117}

Chapter Nine

August Appearance

Several days later, on August 19, Lucia, Francisco, and his older brother John were tending the sheep not far from their house. As they watched the sheep, Lucia noticed a sudden coolness in the air. She saw that Francisco had noticed too. Believing the Lady was soon to arrive, they urged John to go get Jacinta right away. He refused, but when Lucia offered him some money, he agreed. They watched him intently as he ran toward their house. {W 119; P 95}

A short time later there was the bright flash that always preceded the Lady. Just then Jacinta came running across the field to join them. In a moment they saw the Lady standing over an evergreen like the one in the Cova over which she had appeared before. {W 120; P 96}

"What is it you want of me?" Lucia asked. {W 120; P 96}

"I want you to continue to go to the Cova on the thirteenth of the month and continue to recite the Rosary every day," she said. "In the last month I will perform a miracle so that all will believe." Then she added, "Had they not taken you to the town, the miracle would be better known. The child Jesus will come with St. Joseph to bless the world. And Our Lord will come to give peace to the world." {W 120; P 96, 97}

"Several sick people have asked me to beg you to cure them," Lucia asked. {P 97}

"Yes, some I will cure during the year," Our Lady replied. After a brief silence, she said with a sense of urgency, "Pray, pray a great deal, and make sacrifices for sinners. Many souls go to hell because they have no one to sacrifice and pray for them." Then she began to move toward the east and disappeared. {W 120}

The children were filled with delight at having seen Mary, especially after the trial they had gone through with the mayor. When they regained their senses, they broke off some branches from the tree where Mary had appeared, and carried them off. Jacinta waved the branch to Lucia's mother, Maria Rosa, when they arrived, saying, "O auntie, we have just seen Our Lady again! ...Look, Our Lady put one foot on this part of the branch, and the other foot on that part." {W 120; P 98, 99}

"Give me that branch, you little fibber," Maria Rosa said. She smelled it and was surprised by the strange scent, so nice, yet so different. She began at that moment to soften her stance against this whole Cova issue. {W 121; P 99}

Later in the day a couple of friends who also doubted the apparitions, stopped by to visit Maria Rosa. She told them, "Jacinta was here a little while ago and said Our Lady appeared again." {P 99}

All of a sudden they look shocked. "What's the matter," asked Maria Rosa. "Are you sick?" {P 99}

"No, but we were just walking back from the fields... when we saw all kinds of colored lights. I said to my sister, 'Those are the same lights the people spoke of on the thirteenth. If this were the thirteenth they would claim it was an apparition of Our Lady!'" They all began to wonder. {P 99, 100}

During the rest of August and into September, the children increased their prayer and looked for more ways to do penance so as to save souls from hell. Once, Lucia came upon a piece of rope on the road and wrapped it around her arm, tying it tight. "Ooh, that hurts... We could tie this around our waists and offer the pain to God." No sooner said than done. The rope was cut in three and each got a prickly little belt to wear around their waists, so they could offer something for sinners. At times it hurt Jacinta so much that she cried. But, when Lucia encouraged her to take it off, Jacinta replied, "No, I want to offer this to God to make up for sin and convert sinners." {P 101, 102}

It seems their efforts were beginning to have a great effect in their lives, especially in Jacinta. She became more calm, more tender and sometimes could see future events. Once when she said three Hail Marys for a woman with a horrible sickness, she got well on the spot. One woman accused the children of being liars and phonies whenever she saw them. Jacinta's response was simply to comment to her two friends, "We must ask Our Lady to convert this woman. She has so many sins which she doesn't confess that she will go to hell!" After they offered sacrifices for her, she never bothered them anymore. {W 122}

Chapter Ten

September Appearance

On September 12, more people than ever began to stream into Fatima. They were mostly poor people, and many had to miss three days of work to make the long trip here to witness the apparition of Mary. The mayor attempted to discourage pilgrims, but his roadblocks were useless. By ten o'clock on September 13 more than thirty thousand people were present, waiting to see the miracle. Many were quite devout[10] praying the rosary on their knees in the field. {W 125; P 103, 104}

Among the crowd were several seminarians[11] and priests. Two of the priests were there because they wanted to satisfy themselves that this was a hoax, another because the bishop of Lisbon sent him to observe these events and report back. {P 104, 105}

---

[10]Devout means prayerful, dedicated to their faith.

[11]A seminarian is a man who is studying to be a priest.

As the children set out for the Cova the roads were packed with people. They could hardly walk through the thick crowd. Some kind men helped them to move along amidst a sea of people asking for cures, some on their knees. "Ask Mary to cure my son who is crippled... Ask her to heal me of tuberculosis... Ask her to cure my deaf son... my blind child." The requests were endless as the children tried to move through the crowds to the apparition site. At last they got to the tree where Mary appeared, and which had been picked almost clean of its leaves by the pilgrims. {P 106, 107; W 125, 126}

Lucia quieted the crowd and announced the rosary. Everyone knelt as Lucia began the rosary and this murmuring crowd became quiet and was transformed into a sea of praying pilgrims. A little after noon, the sun dimmed, and Lucia broke off from the rosary to shout, "There she is! I see her!" The crowd called out, pointing to the approaching bright sphere which traveled gently along until it stopped above the small tree. {P 107, 108}

A small, beautiful cloud came to cover the tree and the children, and what looked like white spheres of light fell from it and faded into nothing as they descended onto the people's outstretched hands. Meanwhile Lucia began with her standard question, "What do you want of me?" {P 108, 109}

Mary replied, "Continue to pray the beads so as to bring about the end of the war... In October Our Lord will come, and so will Our Lady of Sorrows and Our Lady of Mount Carmel.[12] St. Joseph will also come with the Child Jesus to bless the world." Then Mary added, "God is pleased with your sacrifices, but He does not want you to sleep with the rope. Wear it only during the day." {P 108, 109}

Lucia then said, "The people have begged me to ask you many things. There is a deaf-mute who wants to be cured. And there are requests for conversions... and requests for all kinds of cures." {P 109}

"I will cure some within a year," Mary answered, "but not others." {P 109}

Lucia then asked about what to do with the money the pilgrims had left as offerings to Mary and she gave the young shepherd instructions in that regard. After this Lucia made another request: "There are many who say that I am an imposter and that I deserve to be hanged and burned. Please perform a miracle so that all will believe." {P 110}

Mary answered, "Yes, in October I will perform a miracle so that all may believe." Then, she began to move off in the

---

[12] Our Lady of Sorrows and Our Lady of Mount Carmel represent different titles of the same person, Mary, mother of God.

sky as before. As she moved off into the heavens, the sun became bright again. The cloud which surrounded the children vanished, and the shower of little lights ended. {P 110}

The people began to ask Lucia a ton of questions, but there were so many she just heard a big jumble of words. Two priests who came doubting the appearances became convinced that they were real, and they went among the crowd asking what the people saw. They all agreed that they saw just what the two priests saw. (P 111, 112}

Another priest who had been present, Fr. Formigao, was asked by Lisbon church officials to look into these happenings. He came back to Fatima in late September to question the children. He asked them many things, and the children all seemed to answer very well. Then, he returned October 11 with more questions, but at the end of it all, he was convinced they were telling the truth, whether the events were miraculous or not. {W 128, 129, 131, 134}

Chapter Eleven

October Appearance

As October 13 approached, Lucia's mother began to worry. What would happen when the miracle Lucia promised failed to take place? The crowd would be so angry, God only knew what they would do to her poor daughter. She told her daughter, "It is better for us to go and tell everything... If the Lady does not perform the miracle the crowd will kill us." She urged her daughter to go to confession to get ready for death. Lucia agreed to go to confession, "but not for that reason. The Lady will do tomorrow what she has promised." {W 135, P 113}

On the night of October 12 people began arriving at the Cova to see the promised miracle. The pilgrims occupied themselves with prayers and hymns during their all-night wait for the miracle. The weather was cool, rain was expected, and there had been reports that a bomb would be set off during the appearance, but none of this prevented the thousands of pilgrims from coming to see the final apparition of Mary. {P

113}

On the morning of the 13th, when it was time to leave for the Cova, Lucia got her umbrella, since it was raining, and headed for the door to go to join her two cousins. As she did so both her mother and father, who had been listening too much to the gossip of the neighbors against Lucia, proclaimed, "If my daughter is going to die, I want to die with her!" And so the three headed out together toward the house of Francisco and Jacinta. {P 115}

The going was slow due to the huge number of people in the streets and around the Marto house. Even inside the house, the place was filled with people. Mr. Marto, who was not nearly as upset as his poor wife, tried to comfort her with a bit of humor, saying, "My dear, don't worry. Now that the house is full of people, no one else can come in!" {P 115}

As they went to leave, a friend whispered to Manuel Marto, "If I were you I wouldn't go to the Cova. You might get hurt..." Manuel replied, "Thanks, friend, but I think I'll go just the same. I'm really not the least bit afraid for myself and I have no fear about the way it will turn out." {P 116}

They all proceeded out into the heavy rain and began to trudge along in the muddy road. It was a tiresome and slow walk through the rain and the crowds, but finally they came to the Cova. A huge throng of seventy thousand pilgrims were there waiting for them! Umbrellas were everywhere as the three children took up their places. {P 116}

Despite the pouring rain, Lucia was inspired to ask everyone to fold their umbrellas and pray the rosary. Surprisingly, the crowd did just what she said. {P 118}

Once the rosary was completed a priest, who had been there all night, questioned Lucia, "When is the Lady supposed to appear?" {P 118}

"At noon," the young shepherd answered.

He pulled out his watch and said, "It is already noon. Our Lady doesn't lie. Something seems wrong here. We will soon find out."

Several more minutes passed in waiting. The priest looked at his watch once more and said, "It's well past noon. This whole affair is an illusion. Let's all get out of here!" Then he attempted to move the three away from the site but, despite her high regard for priests, Lucia stood firm. {P 118}

"Whoever wants to go may do so, but I'm not going," she shouted decisively. "This land belongs to my father and I have a right to stay here. Our Lady said she was coming. She came before and she will come again this time." The crowd mumbled words of disappointment, but Lucia continued to look for the sign of Mary's coming. {P 118, 119; W 144}

Suddenly Lucia called out, "Silence! Silence! Our Lady is

coming! We have just seen the flash of light!" The Lady made her dramatic entrance at last. {P 119}

The children all knelt, and the people around them could tell by their glowing faces that Mary had arrived. Lucia began again with, "What do you want of me?" She hardly felt the soft rain spraying her face as she looked up at the beautiful lady. {P 120; W 144}

Mary replied, "I want a chapel built here in honor of Our Lady of The Rosary. Let them continue to say the Rosary every day. The war is going to end and the soldiers will soon return home." {P 120; W 144}

"Will you tell me your name?" asked the little girl. {P 120}

"I am the Lady of The Rosary," Mary responded. {P 120}

"I have many favors to ask. Many are asking for cures and conversions," said Lucia. {P 120}

"I will grant some of their prayers, but not all. They must reform their lives and ask forgiveness for their sins." Then Mary's face turned sorrowful as she said, "People must not offend Our Lord anymore. He is already greatly offended." {P 120, 121}

Then, Mary extended her hands and light from them reached up to the sky to where the sun would have been seen if it were not cloudy. As Mary faded into that light, suddenly the rain stopped, the clouds split open, and the sun became visible in the blue sky. Lucia, in ecstasy,[13] and not even aware of what she was saying, called out "Look at the sun!" Everyone was able to do so without hurting their eyes. {W 144, 145; P 123}

The apparition of Mary ended, but then she reappeared as part of an image of the Holy Family, with Jesus and Joseph, representing the Joyful Mysteries of the Rosary. This was seen by Jacinta and Francisco, not just Lucia, who had seen Mary initially. Jesus and Joseph blessed the people. Following this came an image of Mary as our Lady of Sorrows, with Jesus in sorrow, gazing on His poor mother. In this depiction, symbolizing the Sorrowful Mysteries, Jesus again blessed the crowd. In the third image Mary had the appearance of Our Lady of Mount Carmel, wearing a queen's crown, and holding the child Jesus on her lap. Only Lucia saw the latter two images. {W 145; P 124}

Meanwhile, the other children and the crowd were seeing something else. The sun appeared as a kind of flat disk of light, but more of a silver color than its usual yellow. {W 145; P 124} Manuel Marto described what happened next:

---

[13]Ecstasy means literally standing outside oneself. It means the lifting of the soul above the senses due to a deep union with God.

> [The sun] seemed to flicker on and off, first one way, then another. It shot rays in different directions and painted everything in different colors–the trees, the people, the air and the ground. What was most extraordinary was that the sun did not hurt our eyes at all. Everything was still and quiet... At a certain moment the sun seemed to stop and then began to move and to dance until it seemed that it was being detached from the sky and was falling on us. It was a terrible moment! {DM 135, 136}

In fear, many went down on their knees in the mud, some crying out, "Ai, Jesus, we are all going to die here," or "O God, forgive us our sins!" or "Mary, save us!" or "Miracle, Miracle!" Some prayed the Act of Contrition. Then, it stopped and returned zig-zagging upward to its original position and brightness. After this amazing sequence of events the people began to discuss excitedly what they had seen. {W 146; P 127}

At the same time, in Alburitel, some twelve miles away, the townspeople saw the same thing. One atheist of the town, had earlier ridiculed those who had gone to Fatima "to see a young girl." After the miracle one witness wrote, "I saw him tremble from head to foot, and raising his hands to heaven, he fell on his knees in the mud shouting, "Our Lady! Our Lady!" (P 128; W 149)

The miracle of Fatima was not limited to the skies. A woman from Arnal, 22 miles from Fatima, by the name of Maria do Carmo, heard of the Fatima events and told Mary she would travel there four times in her bare feet as a penance to ask for healing. And what a healing she was asking for. Maria had been ill for five years, with what appeared to be tuberculosis, and other serious problems. It had gotten so bad that she could barely eat or sleep. She and her husband had arrived at Fatima in August, after a painful journey. She was suffering miserably in her whole body. Much to their surprise, however, her pain became much reduced just a few moments after arriving. Furthermore, the journey back home was not nearly so painful and once home, her appetite returned. When she made her second visit September 13, she felt even better. {P 129}

Her third visit, October 13 was her greatest challenge, since it was pouring down rain for the entire 22 mile walk. She made it there after much effort, and it was well worth it. This time all her aches and pains and coughing, and other problems disappeared. She was completely healed. Once the miracle of the sun was over, the people gathered around her to hear her story. News of her healing spread through the crowd. {P 129, 130}

As people were marveling at and discussing all that had happened, they noticed something else extraordinary. Their clothes, soaked just fifteen minutes before, had become completely dry. {P 130}

After some time the crowds began to go their way, and the children returned home. The Lady had kept her promise, and wonderfully so. {W 148}

Chapter Twelve

Anti-Catholic Doings

The enemies of the Church could not rest knowing that so many people were totally won over by the miracle. So, on October 23 at night, they went to the Cova to cut down the tree upon which Mary had stood. They took this and many of the religious articles at the site and brought them to Santarem and the next day held a mock procession through the streets. Alas, their efforts to kill the faith of those who believed in the Fatima miracle failed. It only served to extend the belief to more and more people. {DM 158-160}

There was more. Some of the anti-Catholics gave out fliers ridiculing the apparitions and the priests, and inviting people to meet outside the church on Sunday and make fun of the events at Fatima. To protect the children, the pastor sent them to visit a nearby family for the day. When the non-believers–including the mayor of Ourem and a few of his guards–showed up on Sunday, there was just one person besides the organizers. Frustrated by the small numbers, they decided to go off to the Cova anyway. {DM 160-162}

An embarrassing greeting was waiting for them there. A man had tied some donkeys to nearby trees and when the group got there, he tied a bowl to each one's head containing a certain substance which made them bray loudly. The message was that they were acting like donkeys. The local people had also left a meal for the visitors near the apparition tree: mule food! When the atheists began to say things against the faith, some of the locals shouted back "Blessed be Jesus and Mary!" Soon the atheists realized their whole plan had backfired, and they left. {DM 162, 163}

Chapter Thirteen

Postlogue

After all these October happenings, things began to quiet down. Lucia's mother agreed to let her learn to read, as the Blessed Mother had directed, and she and her cousin Jacinta began to attend school in Fatima. {W 155}

Francisco did not go to school, but continued in his way of offering himself for sinners and of consoling Jesus for the sins of the world. He spent more and more time before the tabernacle, or in some quiet place, praying. In late January 1919 he became quite sick. On April 3 he received his first communion–and his last–in his sick bed. The next day, at ten am, Francisco passed from this world. He was not yet ten. {W 157, 158, 162, 166, 167}

Jacinta became sick when Francisco did, but she lingered on longer. She was told by Mary she would "suffer more for love of Our Lord and for the conversion of sinners." {P 134; W 168, 169}

In July 1919 her father brought her to the hospital in

Ourem, but that failed to improve her condition, and it was expensive. So, in late August he brought her home. {W 170-172}

In January 1920 a priest who had become friends with the family through the miracle came to visit. He brought a doctor and his wife to examine Jacinta. Once the doctor did so, he concluded she needed immediate medical care at a hospital in Lisbon, or she would not survive. He was prepared to pay for this. Her parents reluctantly agreed, and her aunt and brother brought her there soon after. {W 176, 177}

The doctors performed an operation on her on February 10. Little Jacinta suffered terribly for the next six days. Then, the pain stopped but she was still very sick. On February 20 she told the nurse she was dying, and asked for the priest to come. He did, and heard her confession. He felt the following morning would be soon enough to bring Communion. It wasn't. That night, at 10:30 pm Jacinta died. She too was just short of her tenth birthday. {181, 182}

Before she died in 1920 Jacinta revealed remarkable statements made by Our Lady. Here are just some of them:

> More souls go to hell because of sins of the flesh than for any other reason. Certain fashions will be introduced that will offend Our Lord very much. Many marriages are not good; they do not please Our

Lord and are not of God. Priests must be pure, very pure. They should not busy themselves with anything except what concerns the Church and souls. The disobedience of priests to their superiors and to the Holy Father is very displeasing to Our Lord. The Blessed Mother can no longer restrain the hand of her Divine Son from striking the world with just punishment for its many crimes.

Tell everybody that God gives graces through the Immaculate Heart of Mary. tell them to ask graces from her, and that the Heart of Jesus wishes to be venerated together with the Immaculate Heart of Mary.

The bishop felt it wise to arrange for Lucia to go off to a school where she would be unknown and protected from the unbelievers and believers alike. Lucia's mother agreed, and so Lucia left her home in 1921 at the age of 14 for her new school in Vilar, some distance away. After finishing her studies, at age 18 she entered the convent of the sisters who had taught her, the Society of St. Dorothy, in 1925. {W 190, 191; FLW 10, 11}

On December 10, 1925 Mary and the child Jesus appeared

to Sister Lucia in her convent room. Jesus spoke first and then Mary explained further the First Saturday devotions: "...I promise to assist at the hour of death, with the graces necessary of salvation, all those who, on the first Saturdays of five consecutive months, confess, receive Holy Communion, recite part of my Rosary, and keep me company for a quarter hour meditating on its mysteries with the intention of offering me reparation." {W 219; LS 36, 37}

On February 15, 1926 the Child Jesus appeared to Lucia to inquire if she had promoted the First Saturdays. She mentioned some problems her confessor had with it. Her Mother Superior indicated she would be happy to promote it, but Lucia's confessor said she could not do it herself. Jesus said, "It is true your Superior alone can do nothing, but with My grace she can do all."

Then at Lucia's request, Jesus eased the time requirements to allow confession within eight days of the First Saturday, and even more time, "provided that, when they receive Me, they are in the state of grace and have the intention of making reparation to the Immaculate Heart of Mary." And, in fact, Jesus said that if they forgot to make that intention, "They can do so at their next confession, taking advantage of the first opportunity to go to Confession." {LS 38}

In 1939 the bishop of Fatima explained further in a formal

document, "The [additional 15 minute] meditation involves one or more mysteries. It may even include all, taken together or separately, according to individual attraction or devotion; but it is preferable to meditate on one mystery each month." {P 157}

Until 1929 Mary's request that Russia be consecrated to her Immaculate Heart was a secret. But, on June 13, 1929, Mary again appeared to Sr. Lucia to tell her she could now reveal this secret. Lucia was praying alone in the chapel late at night when she saw a bright light, and a vision of the Trinity. In the vision, God the Father was seen above the crucifix upon which Jesus hung. At the top of the cross was the Holy Spirit in the form of a dove. A chalice and host were shown with drops of blood falling onto the host and ending in the chalice. Mary herself stood under the right arm of Jesus on the cross. She was holding her immaculate heart. Under the other arm of the cross were the words "grace and mercy." {LS 40-42}

Mary spoke to Lucia, "The moment has come in which God asks the Holy Father, in union with the bishops of the world, to make the consecration of Russia, to my Immaculate Heart, promising to save it by this means..." {LS 42}

In 1948 Lucia received permission to transfer to the

Discalced Carmelites[14] in Coimbra, Portugal, where she remained until her death (on February 13) 2005, a few weeks before her 98th birthday. Francisco and Jacinta were beatified by Pope John Paul II on May 13, 2000. They were canonized by Pope Francis May 13, 2017. {FLW 11}

---

[14]The Discalced Carmelites (discalced means without shoes, signifying poverty) are the Religious Order founded by St. Teresa of Avila in the 16th century. They are a more strict branch of the Carmelite Order.

The Importance of The Rosary

The Rosary is the meeting ground of the uneducated and the learned; the place where simple love grows in knowledge and where the knowing mind grows in love . . . The rosary is the book of the blind, where they see, and there enact the greatest drama of love the world has ever known; it is the book of the simple which initiates them into mysteries and knowledge more satisfying than the education of other men; it is the book of the aged, whose eyes close on the shadow of this world, and open on the substance of the next. The power of the rosary is beyond description." (Archbishop Fulton Sheen, in *The World's First Love*, pp. 188, 189).

In November 1980 Pope John Paul II was interviewed by a group of Catholics in Fulda, Germany. He was asked, "What is going to happen to the Church?"

He answered:

We must prepare ourselves to suffer great trials before

long, such as will demand of us a disposition to give up even life, and a total dedication to Christ and for Christ... With your and my prayer it is possible to mitigate this tribulation, but it is no longer possible to avert it, because only thus can the Church be effectively renewed. How many times has the renewal of the Church sprung from blood! This time, too, it will not be otherwise. We must be strong and prepared, and trust in Christ and His Mother, and be very, very assiduous in praying the Rosary. (from http://www.fatima.org/thirdsecret/fulda.asp)

The divorce rate among couples praying the daily rosary is about one in 500 (*Soul Magazine*, March-April, 1990)

The Rosary, though clearly Marian in character, is at heart a Christocentric prayer. In the sobriety of its elements, it has all the depth of the Gospel message in its entirety, of which it can be said to be a compendium. It is an echo of the prayer of Mary, her perennial Magnificat for the work of the redemptive Incarnation which began in her virginal womb. With the Rosary, the Christian people sits at the school of Mary and is led to contemplate the beauty on the face of Christ and to experience the depths of his love. Through the Rosary the faithful receive abundant grace, as though from the very hands of the Mother of the Redeemer. (Pope St. John Paul II, *Rosarium Virginis Mariae*, 2002, n. 1)

Rosary should be considered as one of the best and most efficacious prayers in common that the Christian family is invited to recite. We like to think, and sincerely hope, that when the family gathering becomes a time of prayer, the Rosary is a frequent and favored manner of praying. (Bl. Pope Paul VI, *Marialis Cultus*, 1974, n. 54)

Pope St. John Paul II spoke of the rosary as "my favorite prayer."

In saying the rosary, truth sinks into the subconscious like a slow and heavy downpour. The hammered sentences of the gospel receive an indelible validity for precisely the little ones, the least, to whom belongs the Kingdom of Heaven . . . The Rosary is a long and persevering gaze, a meditation, a quieting of the spirit in the praise of God, the value of which we

Protestants are learning once more. (Richard Baumann, German Lutheran Minister in the early 1970's, from *Fatima: The Great Sign*, by Francis Johnston, 2010)

Reflection

The miracle of our Lady at Fatima provided to the world a wonderful introduction to the entire spiritual life. The account of Lucia's first Communion was a great example of the beauty and importance of this event in the life of a child. The appearance of the angel was a reminder of these wonderful helpers and his adoration of the Eucharist was a reminder of the great reverence we should show this wonderful sacrament, truly the body and blood of Jesus. The comment of Our Lady on the children's friend Amelia and her long stay in Purgatory was a reminder of the often-forgotten dogma of purgatory.

Mary also taught the children of the importance of accepting suffering and offering sacrifices for the conversion of sinners. And, they responded generously. Mary showed the children a vision of hell during her third visit, and this was a vivid reminder that hell is real and the suffering there is truly terrible. That vision was also an incentive for the children (and us) to offer sacrifices that sinners might be converted and avoid hell. And, of course, Mary taught the children and the world that we should pray the Rosary daily for world peace. She also pointed out that God wanted to encourage devotion to Mary's Immaculate Heart to save sinners. And, she asked for the consecration of Russia to her Immaculate Heart and the Communion of reparation on the First Saturdays.

Lucia declared in a letter that Pope John Paul II had taken care of consecrating Russia to the Immaculate Heart of Mary when he united with the bishops throughout the world on March 25, 1984, to make "the consecration as Our Lady requested."[15] The fulfilling of Mary's request for the First Saturday devotions is up to us. In fact, it is said that our practice of these devotions is very much related to the conversion of Russia. {P 159}

It seems that when enough people in the world pray the daily rosary, we will have peace in the world. And, when enough people fulfill the First Saturday devotions, Russia will be converted. Will we do as Our Lady asked?

---

[15] See "Letters of Sr. Lucia Santos, OCD on the Consecration," at www.ewtn.com/expert/answers/Fatima1984.

Sources

The Message of Fatima: Lucia Speaks, (identified as "LS" in paragraph references) edited by John Hauf, Washington, NJ: AMI Press, 1997.

DeMarchi, John, IMC, *Fatima: The Full Story*, (identified as "DM" in paragraph references) Washington, NJ: AMI Press, 1985.

Fatima in Lucia's Own Words, Sr. Lucia's Memoirs, vol. I, (identified as "FLW" in paragraph references) edited by Louis Kondor, SVD, Fatima, Portugal: Postulation Center, 1976.

Madigan, Leo, *The Children of Fatima*, (identified as "M" in paragraph references) Huntington, IN: Our Sunday Visitor, 2003.

Pelletier, Joseph, A.A., *The Sun Danced at Fatima*, (identified as "P" in paragraph references) New York: Doubleday, 1983.

"The Message of Fatima," Congregation for The Doctrine of the Faith, (identified as "CDF" in paragraph references) in L'Osservatore Romano, Weekly Edition in English, 28 June 2000, special insert.

Walsh, William Thomas, *Our Lady of Fatima*, (identified as "W" in paragraph references) New York: Doubleday, 1954.

Questions for Discussion

1. Before her first Communion, Lucia prayed before a statue of Mary. What did she ask her?

2. During his second visit to the children, the angel said, "With all your power offer a sacrifice in reparation for the sinners by whom he is offended and of prayer for the conversion of sinners." What does reparation mean? What does conversion mean? Can we too offer prayers and sacrifices for the conversion of sinners?

3. The third time the angel appeared to them he held up a host and chalice and said, "Take and drink the body and blood of Jesus Christ, terribly insulted by ungrateful men." Was that the Eucharist? Was it really the body and blood of Jesus or was that just a symbol?

4. In her first appearance, Mary told Lucia that her friend Amelia would be in purgatory until the end of the world. What is purgatory?

5. Mary told the children that many souls go to hell because others fail to do what?

6. What were some of the sacrifices the children made to make reparation for sins and to convert sinners?

7. What devotion did the Lord want to encourage through Mary's appearances to the three children?

8. The children received a great grace to see Our Lady. Did this bring them praise from the people, or scorn? What might this teach us?

9. Mary told the children to continue to pray so that the war might end. Does this mean our prayers can affect wars?

10. After the final apparition, Francisco spent more and more of his time where? What does this tell us about the best place to pray?

By the Same Author:

Christian Dating in A Godless World (Sophia Institute Press)- The only guide for single Roman Catholics that covers it all, from where to find a good spouse to planning the wedding.
Preview it at www.ccourtship.org.

Be Holy: A Catholic's Guide to the Spiritual Life (Servant Books) - The shortest way to the Kingdom, using the lives and words of the saints.
What Saint Francis de Sales did for his generation, Fr. Morrow does for ours [in Be Holy*].*
–Mike Aquilina

Achieving Chastity in A Pornographic World - A practical guide as to how to break free from addiction to lust and to find peace in the virtue of chastity. Shows you how not only to avoid sexual sins, including pornography, but also to do it joyfully.

Who's Who in Heaven: Real Saints for Families - (Emmaus Road) 11 fascinating saints stories parents can read to their children.

Overcoming Sinful Anger: How to Master Your Emotions and Bring Peace to Your Life (Sophia Institute Press) - Practical ways to conquer anger with the advice of Sacred Scripture and The Lives of the Saints.

A Disciple's Way of The Cross (Stations) - Preview at www.cfalive.com.

World's Most Powerful Mysteries - Revised Edition with 20 Mysteries, Rosary Meditations in Poetry and Sacred Scripture - Preview at www.cfalive.com.

Free Rosary recording with Handel's Messiah in the background from our web site, www.cfalive.org. Click on Rosary recording and follow instructions to download 8 mp3 files to phone or burn a CD.

For these and other booklets, leaflets and other writings by the author, go to www.cfalive.org.

Made in the USA
Middletown, DE
10 May 2017